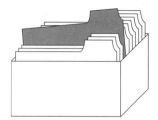

# Contents

## Preparing the Presentation

## Putting it into Words

## Evaluating the Presentation

# About this book

This book is divided into three sections.

## Preparing the presentation

These chapters give advice and hints about presentation skills.

## Putting it into words

In this section of the book, you will find useful advice to help you with the language you need to give an effective presentation.

## Evaluating the presentation

This section consists of checklists that you can use to evaluate your presentation.


# Use of symbols in this book

This warning symbol indicates common problems and important points.

This indicates additional information worth noting.

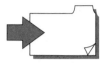

This refers to other chapters or sections with relevant information.

This symbol indicates important cultural points.

This symbol is used to indicate a 'hint' or suggestion to improve your presentation.

This indicates important points you should think about when you are giving the presentation.

# Preparing the Presentation

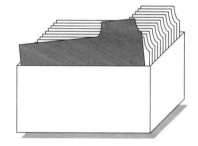

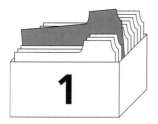

# Introduction

When planning a presentation, the main factors to consider are:

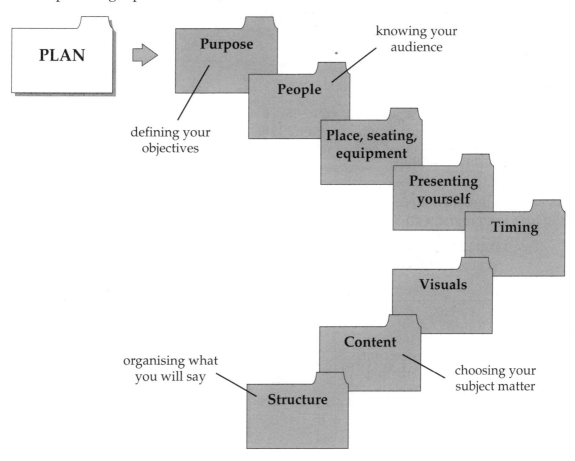

PLAN

Purpose

defining your objectives

People

knowing your audience

Place, seating, equipment

Presenting yourself

Timing

Visuals

Content

choosing your subject matter

Structure

organising what you will say

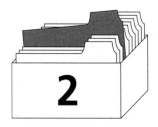

# Purpose

## 2

When planning your presentation, you should decide on the **purpose** or objective of the presentation. Once you have defined your objectives, you can plan how to achieve them by preparing the content of your presentation more precisely.

## Defining objectives

Don't just think about the subject of your speech, think about what you wish to achieve at the end of the presentation. Ask yourself, **'Why am I giving this presentation?' (purpose or objective)**, as well as, **'What am I going to talk about?' (subject)**. Having a clear purpose will help you prepare what you will say and how you will say it.

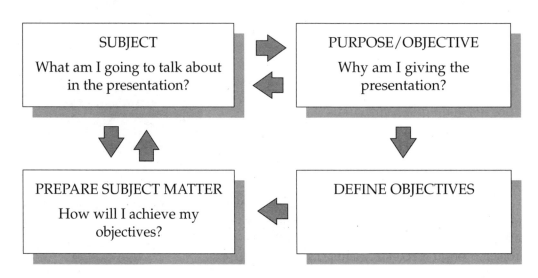

SUBJECT

What am I going to talk about in the presentation?

PURPOSE/OBJECTIVE

Why am I giving the presentation?

PREPARE SUBJECT MATTER

How will I achieve my objectives?

DEFINE OBJECTIVES

# Achieving your objectives

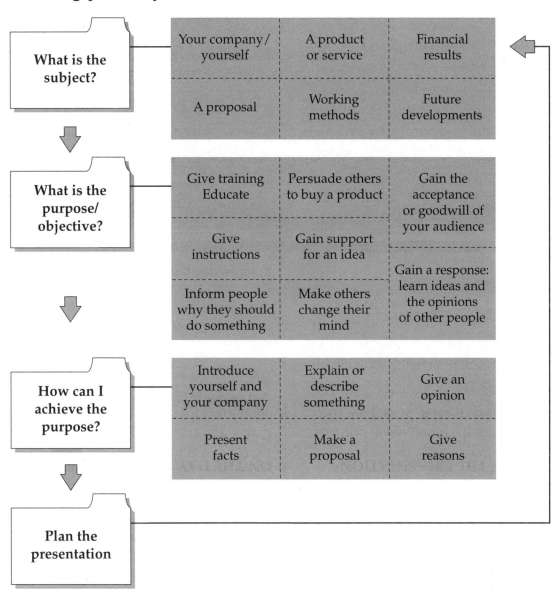

| | | |
|---|---|---|
| **What is the subject?** | | |
| Your company / yourself | A product or service | Financial results |
| A proposal | Working methods | Future developments |

| | | |
|---|---|---|
| **What is the purpose/ objective?** | | |
| Give training Educate | Persuade others to buy a product | Gain the acceptance or goodwill of your audience |
| Give instructions | Gain support for an idea | Gain a response: learn ideas and the opinions of other people |
| Inform people why they should do something | Make others change their mind | |

| | | |
|---|---|---|
| **How can I achieve the purpose?** | | |
| Introduce yourself and your company | Explain or describe something | Give an opinion |
| Present facts | Make a proposal | Give reasons |

**Plan the presentation**

## Evaluating your performance

Afterwards, you can evaluate your presentation and assess whether you achieved exactly what you wanted and if not, why not.

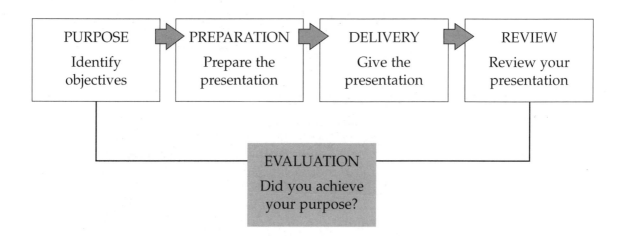

See section on *Evaluating the Presentation* (Chapters 33-35).

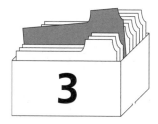

# People

When you give a presentation you should think about the people you will be talking to - the **audience**. The tone, formality, technical content and style of your presentation will depend on who these people are.

## Identity

You may know in advance exactly who is in your audience. If not, try find out as much as possible beforehand.

WHO ARE THEY?

## Audience's aims

The audience will be interested to hear what you have to say and will want to listen to you for a **reason**.

What you want to achieve from the presentation (your purpose) should be consistent with what you think your audience is expecting. If you talk about something that the audience doesn't want to know, your presentation will not be a success.

WHY ARE THEY HERE?

## Numbers/formality

The size of the group will determine the formality of your presentation. For a large audience sitting in rows, a formal presentation will be necessary. For a smaller group sitting around a table, the presentation can be much more informal.

Greater formality is required for an 'external' audience than for an 'internal' audience of colleagues. For example, an important sales presentation to a large client will be more formal than a small presentation to your colleagues who know you well.

See Chapter 4, *Place, Seating and Equipment*.

## Knowledge

You should consider the **level of knowledge** that your audience has about the subject of your presentation when you plan the content of your talk.

Don't waste time telling your audience what they know already or annoy them by assuming that they know more than they do.

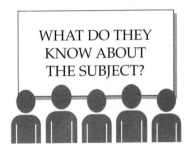

When you give an informal presentation to a small audience, you can ask them how much they know. You can then adjust the content of your presentation if they know more or less than you were expecting. This is not possible in a formal presentation.

If you are talking about a technical matter to non-experts, try to cut down on 'jargon', technical terms and acronyms. Explain such terms clearly and simply.

## Attitude

In most cases, your audience will be friendly and interested in what you have to say. Occasionally, your audience will be unfriendly. This may occur if the audience has strong opinions about the subject of your presentation.

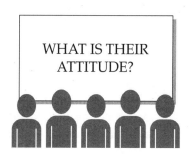

Try to anticipate the problem and plan your presentation in a way that will improve the attitude of the audience to you and what you will be saying. You can do this by presenting controversial topics in a diplomatic way.

### Negative attitudes

| **Example: aggression** | **Example: suspicion** |
| --- | --- |
| At an internal presentation to employees, there may be **resentment** over reorganisation plans in the company. | There may be **mistrust** between employees and management over plans to change working practices. |

# Relationship with the audience

Think of the audience as a group of **individuals**, rather than as a whole group together. If the audience likes you, they will probably be more willing to listen to what you say and may be more willing to agree with your ideas and proposals.

Here are some things to consider that may help you develop a good relationship with the audience.

## Culture

The audience may come from a different cultural background. This might affect the style and structure of your presentation.

| Example: humour | Example: questions and answers |
|---|---|
| British and American presenters and audiences appreciate humour. You should often try and relax the audience by telling a joke. However, this is not true of all cultures. | Some presenters like to ask the audience questions during the presentation. However, in some cultures, people in the audience will refuse to answer and will perhaps be annoyed that a question has been asked. They expect you to do the talking. |

## Language

Other non-native speakers of English in the group may not have the same level of English as you. You may need to speak more slowly than usual. Avoid using idioms and keep the language clear and simple.

You could provide short notes and **handouts** for the audience to refer to to help them understand what you are trying to say.

## Inspire confidence

The audience needs to have confidence in you as a presenter, otherwise they may not have confidence in what you have to say. Here are four ways in which the presenter can encourage confidence:

- know your subject extremely well
- have a positive attitude
- speak clearly
- be confident and look confident

See Chapter 5, *Presenting Yourself.*

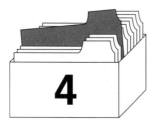

# Place, seating, equipment

**4**

To make sure that your presentation goes as smoothly as possible, try to arrive early and familiarise yourself with the

- place
- seating arrangements
- equipment

You may wish to ask questions about the room where you will be giving the presentation. You can telephone the conference or presentation organisers beforehand. Usually they make all the arrangements but you may be able to make some changes if you wish. For example, it might be possible to alter the seating arrangement or to obtain some equipment that you would like to use.

## The place

Here are some things that you should check:

### Size of the room

Check whether the room is large or small and how many people will be in your audience. A large room filled with rows of people will require a more formal arrangement than if you are giving your presentation to one or two people in a small room. A large group of people seated in a small room may be uncomfortable and you will have to work hard to keep their attention. These factors can affect the type of presentation you choose to give.

# ROOM SIZE AND SIZE OF AUDIENCE

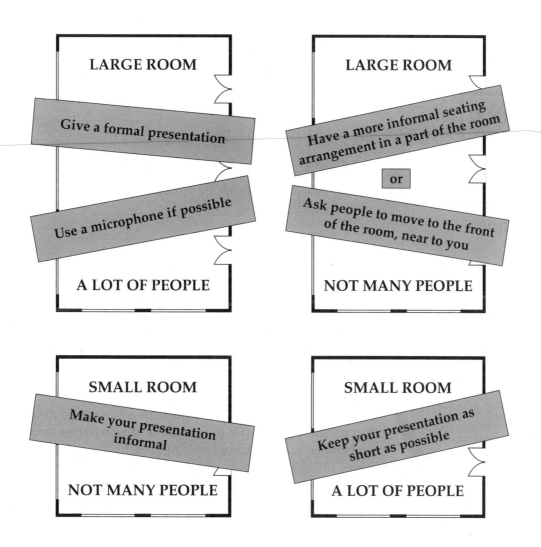

**LARGE ROOM**

Give a formal presentation

Use a microphone if possible

**A LOT OF PEOPLE**

**LARGE ROOM**

Have a more informal seating arrangement in a part of the room

or

Ask people to move to the front of the room, near to you

**NOT MANY PEOPLE**

**SMALL ROOM**

Make your presentation informal

**NOT MANY PEOPLE**

**SMALL ROOM**

Keep your presentation as short as possible

**A LOT OF PEOPLE**

The size of the room affects how much you need to **project your voice**. Remember that when the room is large, you will need to speak more loudly than normal. Check whether there is a **microphone** and, if possible, practise using it.

## Where will you stand?

Check how much space you have to move around when you answer questions or operate equipment.

You should **face the audience** most of the time during a presentation. Is this possible in your position?

## Where will you put your notes?

Check if there is a **table** on which to put your notes, visuals, handouts and other aids. If the presentation is quite long, you will probably want somewhere to put a glass of water.

## Position of the equipment

Check the position of the equipment supplied by the presentation organiser. You should be able to reach it easily. This will depend on the type of equipment you are using.

If you are using a flip chart, place it so that you can write on it without turning your back on the audience.

If you bring your own equipment, check that it is suitable for the place. A flip chart is useless in a large room because people at the back of the room will not be able to read your notes.

## Lighting

Think about the **lighting** you need for certain equipment. An image projected on to a screen may not show up in a brightly lit room. This is a common mistake. If you are using a **projector** (an overhead projector, a data projector or a slide projector) or if you are showing a **film**, it is very important that your audience should be able to see the image clearly. They will not be able to do this if there is too much light in the room.

### Before you begin the presentation

| | | |
|---|---|---|
| Test the equipment. Can you see the image clearly? | If you cannot, try to make the room darker. Turn out the lights or cover the windows. | If you still cannot see the image clearly, you have a problem. Is it too late to use a different room? |

## Seating arrangements

Sometimes, as a presenter, you may be able to decide on the seating arrangements for your audience. You can contact the presentation organiser beforehand. Think about the **size of the group**. It is possible to create either an **informal** or a **formal** atmosphere with seating arrangements.

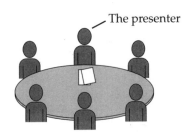

**For a very small group of people, you may prefer to have an informal arrangement, perhaps with everyone sitting around the same table.**

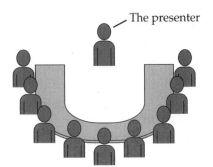

**For a slightly larger group, it can be helpful to have people sitting in a 'U' shape, rather like a horseshoe.** This is less formal than having people sit one behind the other. They can all see the presenter clearly and each other, making communication easier.

**For very large groups of people, there is no alternative to having the audience sitting in a rather formal arrangement in rows.**

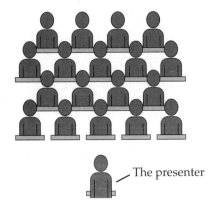

# Types of equipment

There are various types of **equipment** you can use to show visuals. Some are used with visuals that you **prepare in advance**. Others can be used to create visuals **during the presentation** itself.

Sometimes, presenters use **flip charts** or **whiteboards** to create visuals during a presentation. Occasionally, flip charts are used to show visuals that have been prepared in advance. Visuals can also be presented on **pin boards** in the room.

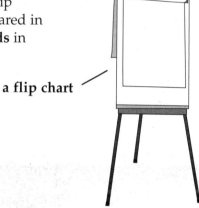

**a flip chart**

**a whiteboard**

---

✓ **CHECK** that any visuals you create on a flip chart or whiteboard can be seen at the back of the room.

**CHECK** that you have enough pens and that the pens work.

---

Many people give presentations using a **computer**. The visuals are prepared using a presentation software package and are then projected on to a screen by a **video data projector** or a **tablet** (a flat glass panel which is plugged into a computer).

**a video data projector**
(for computer presentations)

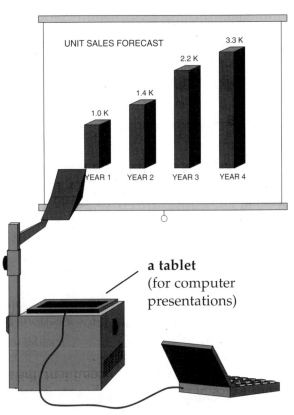

✓ **CHECK** that the software with which you created your presentation is compatible with that on the machine, that the projector is focused and the lighting in the room is suitable.

**a tablet**
(for computer presentations)

One of the most common methods of showing visuals is the **overhead projector**. Pre-prepared **transparencies** are projected on to a **screen**. Visuals can be created during the presentation by drawing on a roll of transparent film.

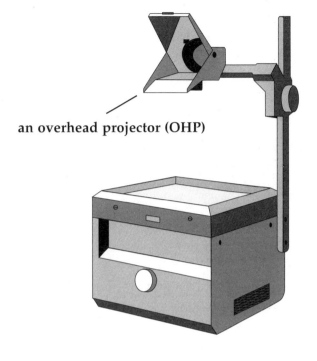

**an overhead projector (OHP)**

 **CHECK** that there is a spare bulb in the projector, that the image fills the screen and not the wall, that transparencies are readable from the back of the room, that the projector is focused and that the lighting in the room is suitable.

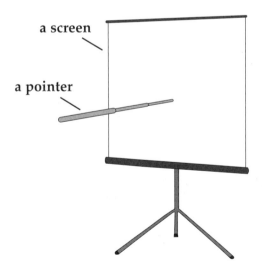

a screen

a pointer

A **screen** will be needed for a video data projector, an overhead projector or a slide projector.

You may wish to use a **pointer** for pointing at items on the screen.

**Photographic slides** can be projected on to a screen using a **slide projector**.

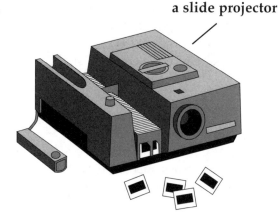

a slide projector

 **CHECK** that photographic slides are in the right order and the right way up, that the projector is focused and the lighting in the room is suitable.

You may need to use a **microphone** if you are giving a presentation to a large audience.

a microphone

 **CHECK** whether it is one that clips on to your clothes or is fixed. (If it is a fixed microphone, you will need to stand at a fixed distance from the microphone.)

## Choosing the equipment

You should consider which type of equipment will be the most suitable for your presentation. Each method of showing visuals has some advantages (and disadvantages) and is suitable for particular uses. Some of these are listed on the next page.

| EQUIPMENT | ADVANTAGES |
|---|---|
| **Flip chart/ whiteboard** | Visuals can be prepared in advance. Visuals can be created during the presentation. |
| **Overhead projector and transparencies** | Visuals are easy to prepare in advance and can look neat and professional. **Masking** can be used to hide the content and then to reveal one piece of information at a time during your presentation.<br><br>You can use a combination of prepared transparencies and visuals created during the presentation.<br><br>A large image can be projected on to a screen. |
| **Video data projector/ tablet and computer-generated graphics** | You can produce high quality graphics with colour and animation. These can be projected on to a large screen.<br><br>In some cases, you can alter the content of a visual during your presentation. For example, numbers can be altered in a spreadsheet. |
| **Slide projector and slides** | Pictures/photographs can convey a strong message and provoke a response from the audience, for example, showing a building project that has taken many years, at the beginning and the end or the devastation caused by natural disaster.<br><br>Any image can be made into a slide. |
| **Film** | A film can create a long-lasting impression on the audience.<br><br>(Film is not often used in presentations because it can take your audience's attention away from what you are saying to them.) |

# Checking equipment

The presentation organiser should check the equipment for you. However, you should always check it yourself. There is nothing more embarrassing than switching something on in the middle of a presentation only to find that it is not working. You should also beware of electric wires lying on the floor, you might trip over one during your talk!

| **BEFORE THE PRESENTATION** | **ON THE DAY** |
|---|---|
| Check with the presentation organiser whether you need to bring your own equipment.<br><br>Choose equipment that is suitable for the venue and plan your presentation using it. | Check that you have all the equipment that you need and that it is in good working order. <br><br>Do your pens work? Do you need a new pen? Do you have enough colours?<br><br>Practise using the equipment. |

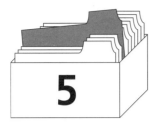

# Presenting yourself

To make a good impression on your audience, it is not just what you say that is important. The way that you say it is important too.

- **What you say.** This is the content of your presentation. Planning the content is an important part of the preparation for giving a presentation. It is dealt with in Chapter 11.

- **How you say it.** Your audience will notice the way you use your voice and your body language. This will affect the way they listen to what you have to say. This is dealt with in Chapters 6 and 7.

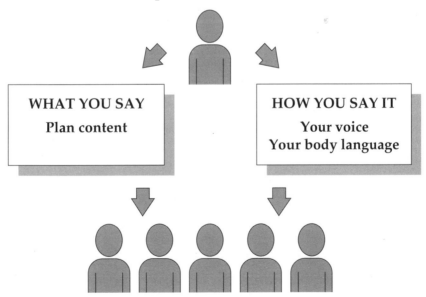

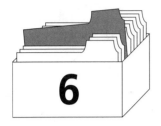

**6**

# Using your voice

You need to think about these things:

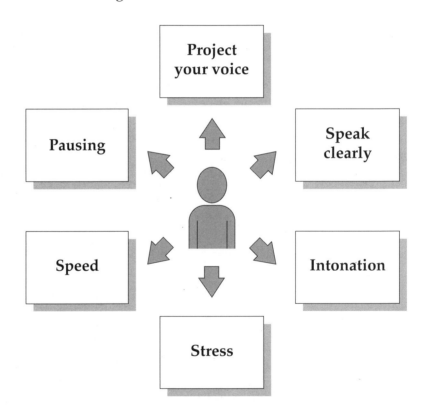

## Project your voice

When giving a presentation you will have to speak more loudly than in a normal conversation. The size of the room and whether or not there is a microphone will determine how much you need to project your voice.

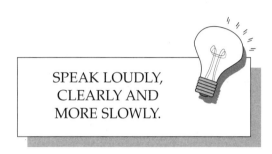

SPEAK LOUDLY, CLEARLY AND MORE SLOWLY.

## Speak clearly

Try to speak clearly. If there are other non-native speakers listening, speak more slowly than normal.

## Intonation and stress

English is a language in which the tone of your voice and the stress that you place on words and sentences is important. Getting the stress and intonation wrong can affect people's understanding of your message.

Listen to native speakers as often as you can or listen to cassettes of native speakers, and practise copying their intonation and stress.

## Intonation

You should **vary the tone** of your voice. Intonation patterns vary between languages. What is normal in your own language may sound uninteresting, monotonous or even aggressive in another. Here are some examples of intonation patterns in **English**:

**Example 1: voice falls**

The voice usually falls at the end of a statement (but this is not always the case as you may wish to stress certain words to alter the emphasis).

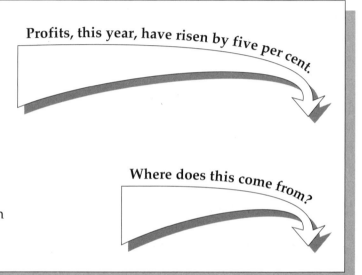

**Example 2: voice falls**

The voice usually falls at the end of an 'open' question (with 'What', 'Who', 'When', 'Why', 'Where', 'Which', 'How').

**Example: voice rises**

The voice rises at the end of a 'closed' question (those requiring the answers 'Yes' and 'No').

## Word stress

English is a 'stress-timed' language. This means that different syllables have a different amount of stress. Many other languages are 'syllable-timed', each syllable having the same amount of stress. People whose first language is syllable-timed can sometimes sound monotonous in English if they give each syllable an equal amount of stress.

Think about some of the key words that you want to use in your presentation. Learn the word stress by listening to a native speaker or by looking in a monolingual (English-English) dictionary. It is helpful to write down important words, marking the stress, like this:

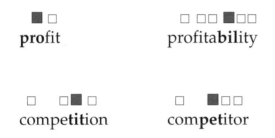

Word stress remains the same wherever the word appears in the sentence. There is a regular pattern to each word and once you have learnt this pattern, you will never need to change it.

## Sentence stress

Sentence stress varies according to the meaning you want to convey.

Stress is placed on the most important words in a sentence and can change the emphasis of what is being said. Look at this sentence said in four different ways:

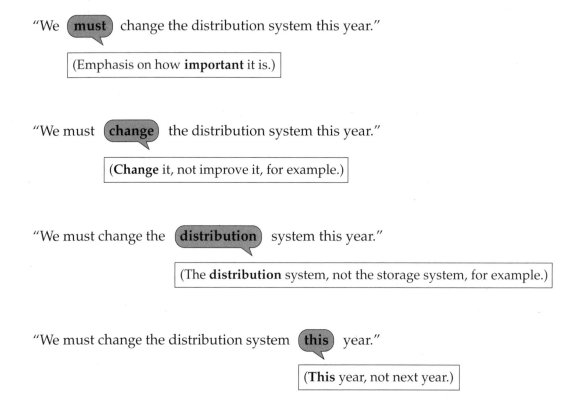

"We **must** change the distribution system this year."

(Emphasis on how **important** it is.)

"We must **change** the distribution system this year."

(**Change** it, not improve it, for example.)

"We must change the **distribution** system this year."

(The **distribution** system, not the storage system, for example.)

"We must change the distribution system **this** year."

(**This** year, not next year.)

Think about the message that you want to give to the audience. Ask yourself which words you will need to emphasise and practise before the presentation.

## Speed

When people give presentations, they speak more slowly than usual. If you slow down too much, the audience may get bored and stop listening. On the other hand, if you speak too quickly, it can be difficult for people to understand what you are saying.

Presenters sometimes increase their speed a little when they want to excite the audience and slow down for emphasis but don't 'overdo' either of these techniques.

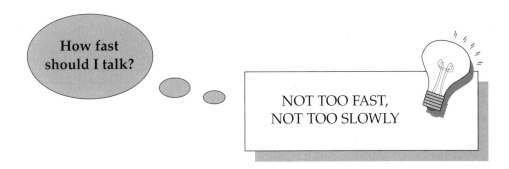

## Pausing

Natural pausing happens in all speech and it is usual to pause at the end of a sentence. We also pause after a '**sense group**'. This is a group of words which belong together, often a clause in a longer sentence. Here is an example:
However, you can also use pauses in other places to emphasise important points of

Our subsidiary companies ‖ PAUSE ‖ of which there are

four ‖ PAUSE ‖ all performed extremely well last year.

your presentation. Here are some examples:

- to give the  audience time to absorb or analyse what you have just said
- to create a break between topics
- to focus the audience's attention on a visual
- to add drama when discussing a controversial or emotional subject

The audience will expect you to pause naturally during your speech. Don't be afraid to use a pause to give you time to think about what your next point should be.

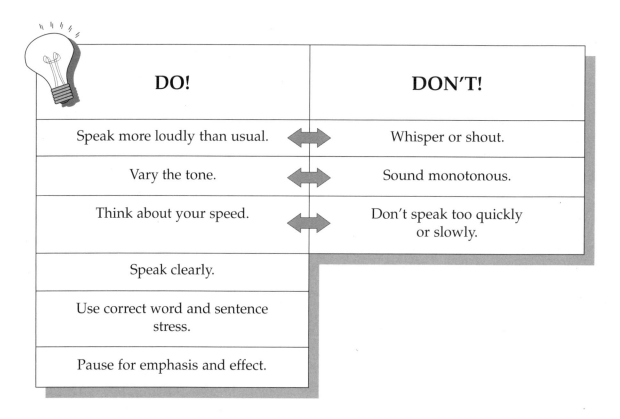

| DO! | DON'T! |
|---|---|
| Speak more loudly than usual. | Whisper or shout. |
| Vary the tone. | Sound monotonous. |
| Think about your speed. | Don't speak too quickly or slowly. |
| Speak clearly. | |
| Use correct word and sentence stress. | |
| Pause for emphasis and effect. | |

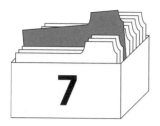

# Body language

**7**

Most people giving a presentation think a lot about the words they are going to use. What they often forget is that we also communicate without speaking. We transmit our feelings and attitudes through body language and non-verbal signals such as gestures and facial expressions.

The audience will read your body language and make judgements about you. They might interpret different meanings behind your words. You should be aware of this so that you don't create a bad impression of yourself.

You need to think about these things:

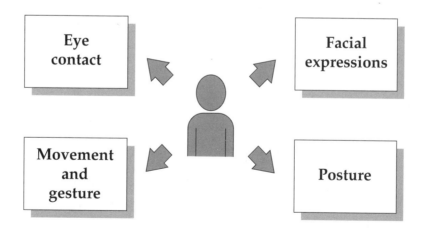

Eye contact

Facial expressions

Movement and gesture

Posture

# Eye contact

## MAINTAINING EYE CONTACT

When giving a presentation, you should try to **maintain eye contact with the audience**. This helps to establish rapport with the audience because it shows that you are interested in them. In return, they will have a positive attitude towards you.

Look around at different members of the audience and do not just focus on people sitting in one particular area. When an individual member of the audience asks a question, you should look at him or her.

## AVOIDING EYE CONTACT

**In most western cultures** it is considered important to maintain eye contact when you are speaking or listening to another person. **Avoiding eye contact** can be interpreted as a sign of insincerity. It is also a sign of nervousness. The audience may lose confidence in you as a presenter and consequently in the content of your presentation.

**In some cultures**, too much eye contact is considered to be a sign of disrespect. If you are unsure about the correct behaviour, contact the conference or presentation organiser.

### Example of bad eye contact

Some presenters look down and read every word of their speech from their notes, never establishing eye contact with the audience. Avoid this at all costs. It is better to make brief notes on cards which you can glance at quickly from time to time.

## Facial expressions

On first impression, we often judge a person's attitude and character by his or her facial expression and when an audience is listening to a presentation, they will study the presenter's face. It is therefore important to maintain a **positive and pleasant facial** expression. If you look relaxed and confident, the audience will have a positive feeling about you.

Most business presentations have a serious purpose but you can **smile**. A smile creates empathy with the audience and will possibly make you feel more relaxed. Smile also when you answer questions.

Try not to let your facial expression betray your emotions if someone in the audience irritates you. The audience will respect you more if you remain calm.

## Posture

Unless you are giving a very informal presentation to a very small audience, it is better to **stand up**, rather than to sit.

- The audience will be able to see you clearly.
- You will be able to see the audience's reactions.
- You can project your voice better.
- You won't have to keep standing up to deal with visuals.

# Movement and gesture

Unnecessary movements and gestures can take the attention of your audience away from the words you are saying. They can also make you look nervous and give the audience the impression that you lack confidence.

## MOVING ABOUT

Some presenters like to move close to the audience during the presentation. This could be a bad idea. In general, it is less distracting for the audience if you **stay in one place** except when you need to move in order to operate equipment or deal with visuals.

For example, there is a tendency for some presenters to walk towards the middle of a U-shaped ('horseshoe') audience. This means that members of the audience seated at either end of the 'U' become excluded and can only see the presenter's back.

## HANDS AND ARMS

When presenters feel nervous, they sometimes fold their arms in front of their bodies in a defensive position or they clasp their hands together very tightly. There is a risk that the audience may interpret this body language negatively.

**Do not fiddle nervously** with slides, pointers and other pieces of equipment. If you do this, the audience will concentrate on what you are doing and will not listen to what you have to say.

Here are some suggestions about how to adopt a natural, relaxed position:

- Clasp hands loosely together in front of you.
- Rest hands by your sides.
- Hold something, e.g. a pen or your note cards in one hand.
- Place one hand on a corner of the podium or equipment.

| DO! | | DON'T! |
|---|---|---|
| Think about eye contact. | ⬌ | Look at the floor or ceiling or down at your notes all the time. |
| Use notes (on cards) to jog your memory. | ⬌ | Read aloud from your notes. |
| Stay in one place. | ⬌ | Move around nervously. |
| Stand still. | ⬌ | Make unnecessary gestures. |
| Stay at the front of the room. | ⬌ | Walk towards the middle of the audience. |
| Have a positive facial expression. | ⬌ | Look negative. |
| | | Fiddle with equipment. |

# Timing

## 8

You will need to plan your talk in order to keep to the time available. Most audiences become restless and impatient if a speaker talks for too long.

## Length

The length of a presentation is usually decided by the presentation organiser. When you are planning your presentation, remember that, generally, audiences find it difficult to sit and listen to someone for more than about **thirty minutes** at a time, without being able to respond or ask questions.

## Content

There are two ways you can plan the content and length of your presentation. Ask yourself:

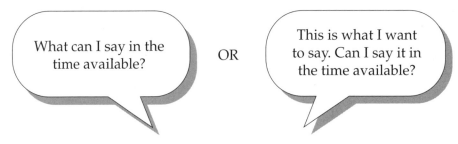

What can I say in the time available?

OR

This is what I want to say. Can I say it in the time available?

The same general principles apply for both methods.

Don't try to say more than you have time for. In a presentation of five minutes or less, you might only be able to cover a few points.

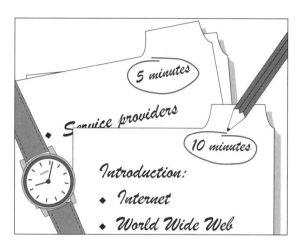

Decide how long each part of the presentation should take in minutes. Mark this time on your notes.

Decide beforehand which parts of your presentation are not essential and could be left out if you are taking longer than you expected and you begin to run out of time. You will have to judge this as you speak by referring to a watch or clock. It may help to put a watch on the table next to your notes.

If you try to cover too much information in your presentation, you will run out of time and you will have to rush the last few points. This will spoil your presentation and confuse your audience. You will give a poor impression of yourself.

See Chapter 11, *Content* and Chapter 12, *Structure*.

## Rehearsals

If you have the time, it can be helpful to rehearse your presentation out loud on your own. If possible, ask colleagues to act as an audience. If your talk is going over time, you will have to decide which parts to reduce or leave out.

Rehearsing will also allow you to practise and perhaps make improvements. For example, practise how to emphasise an important point in your presentation. You can do this by **pausing** for a second or two before and after you make the point to allow the audience to think about the message.

See Chapter 5, *Presenting Yourself.*

## Questions

You should allow time for the audience to ask questions after you have finished speaking. You can rehearse answers to possible questions beforehand.

See Chapter 19, *Stating the purpose, giving an outline*, 'Saying when you will deal with questions' and Chapter 31, *Dealing with questions.*

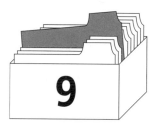

# Preparing visuals

Good visuals will help your audience to understand what you are trying to tell them. They can also make your presentation seem more 'professional' and will help to give the audience confidence in you and your subject.

## How many?

The number of visuals you use will depend on the **subject** or **content** of your presentation and the **time available**. You should allow enough time for the audience to absorb the information on the visual and for you to say what you want to about it.

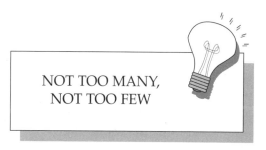

NOT TOO MANY,
NOT TOO FEW

Visuals can sometimes take the attention of your audience away from you. Try not to let them dominate your presentation. However, don't under-use them either. The audience will be kept interested if you move from one visual to the next as you give your presentation.

## Content and design

Keep the content and design of the visuals simple. If your visuals are too complicated, they will confuse the audience.

If they have too much writing on them, the letters may be too small and the visual will be difficult to read.

NOT TOO MUCH
INFORMATION
ON VISUALS

## Key words and phrases

Visuals should be relevant to the content of your presentation. Use the same key words in your visuals that you are using in your talk.

Our aim is to be the **market leader** in the **global communications market**. Our strategy for achieving this aim is to enter **international alliances**.

AIM AND STRATEGY
- Market leader
- Global telecommunications market
- International alliances

## Don't use long sentences

Do not show all the words of your speech on a visual.

- The visual will be very difficult to read.
- The visual should present a **summary** of what you are saying or should **illustrate** the points that you wish to discuss.

> Three years ago, our company began a major project to review and update its computer systems. We wanted to make our systems extremely efficient, using the latest technology.

**INCORRECT**

**CORRECT**

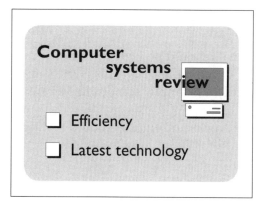

The audience should not have to listen to and read the same information to understand a point. Use your visuals to summarise or show additional information to that which is in your talk. Don't use visuals just to repeat what you are saying.

The visuals are there to help your audience but during the presentation they can also remind **you** of the next point you wish to make.

## Layout

Visuals should be **well-designed**. A clear layout helps the audience to understand what the visual represents. This is the same for visuals which are created in front of the audience, for example, something written on a flip chart.

The words and figures should be large enough for everyone to read them easily.

Try not to put too much information or too many images on to one visual - use two or three visuals, if necessary, instead.

| **A BAD VISUAL** | **BETTER VISUALS** |
|---|---|

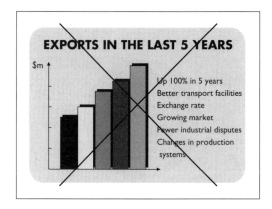

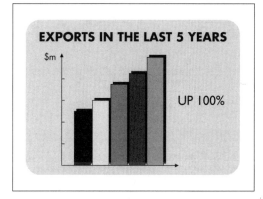

**WHY HAVE EXPORTS INCREASED BY SO MUCH?**

► Better transport facilities

► Exchange rate

► Growing market

► Fewer industrial disputes

► Changes in production systems

### Pictures, charts, colours, symbols

A combination of words and pictures will make your visuals more interesting to the audience.

Where possible use **pictures** or **charts** instead of words or columns of figures.

<table>
<tr><td align="center">NOT SO GOOD</td><td align="center">BETTER</td></tr>
<tr><td>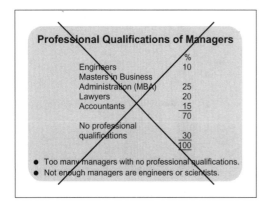</td><td></td></tr>
</table>

Use **colour** and **symbols** to draw attention to important facts or to develop a common theme. You could add your firm's name or logo and the customer's logo at a sales presentation.

# Types of visuals

If you are presenting numbers or statistics (e.g. percentages, profits, etc.), you could use these visuals:

### a bar chart

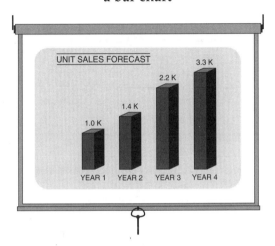

### a pie chart

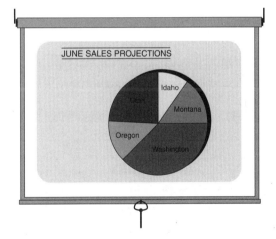

### a graph

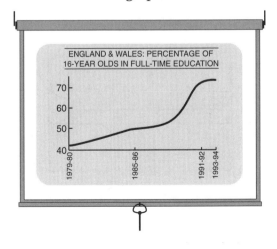

## a table of figures

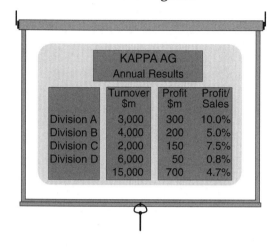

**Flowcharts** are useful to show
a sequence of events.

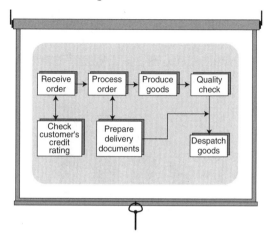

**Organigrams** can be used to
show company structure.

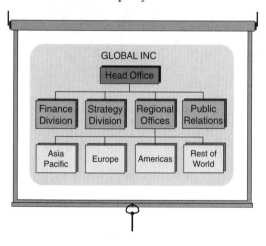

**Plans** are often used to
show locations.

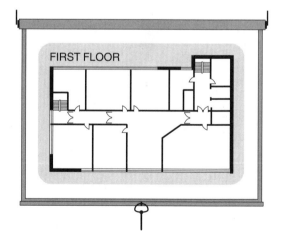

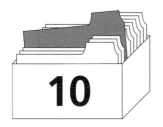

# Using visuals

**10**

In addition to preparing high-quality visuals, a presenter should use the visuals properly. Visuals should help you to deliver your message. They should not take the attention of your audience away from what you are trying to say.

## Be organised

Make sure that your transparencies, slides and other visuals are in the correct order. It will be embarrassing if you cannot find the one you want during the presentation. Your audience will judge you on these mistakes.

If you can do so easily, **switch off the OHP (overhead projector) between visuals**. Do not leave it switched on when there are no visuals.

**Use a pointer** to indicate which part of the visual you wish to refer to. You can use a long pointer to point to the screen or a short one placed on the projector if you are using an overhead projector.

## Talk to the audience, not to the visuals

Visuals are there to be seen! Make sure that you do not stand in front of the screen. Try not to look at the screen if this means that you have to turn your back to the audience. Stand to one side of the screen or flip chart in a position where you can always **face the audience**.

Making a video

Idea
Story
Script
Actors
Filming
Editing

### CREATING VISUALS

Many presenters like to write things on a flip chart or whiteboard when presenting to small groups. Stand to one side of the chart or board when you are writing on it, so that you can still face the audience. Your writing should be larger than normal, clear and legible. Use notes or key words. Do not write long sentences.

## Prepare the audience for the visuals

Before you show your next visual to the audience, it is often helpful to talk about what it will demonstrate.

Make your point, introduce the visual and then put it on the screen. Discuss it with the audience and explain its significance. Visuals cannot explain anything themselves. The explanations must come from you. Always give your audience time to look at the visual before you remove it.

See Chapter 28, *Referring to visuals*.

How long should
I leave a visual
on the screen?

NOT TOO LONG, NOT TOO SHORT

Don't leave a visual on the screen for longer than is necessary as it will distract the audience from your next point. However, don't go immediately on to the next visual before your audience has had time to absorb the information.

# Building up a picture

You can use visuals to reveal information gradually with masks or overlays.

## Masks

If you are using an overhead projector, you should use a **mask** and reveal each piece of information at a time if the information follows a sequence. (A mask can just be a piece of paper!)

By using a mask and 'hiding' the parts that follow, you ensure that everyone is looking at one part of the visual at a time and not reading ahead of you.

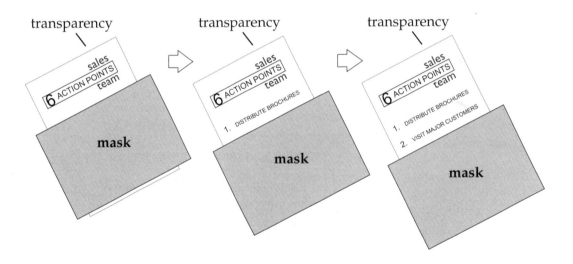

## Overlays

You can use **overlays** to build up a sequence of transparencies. More information is added to the image as each transparency is laid directly over the next.

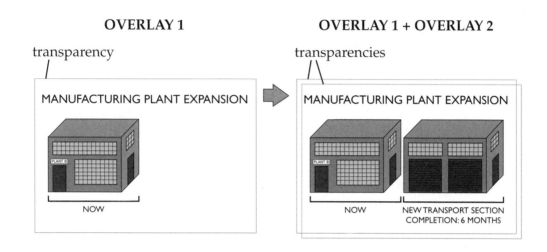

You can create the same effects as masks and overlays with computer presentation software. Bullet points, graphics, etc. can be programmed to appear on screen gradually.

See Chapter 4, *Place, Seating, Equipment*.

| DO! | | DON'T! |
|---|---|---|
| Consider the number of visuals to use. |  | Use too many visuals. |
| Prepare your audience for visuals. |  | Don't show visuals without an introduction |
| Stand to one side of the screen. |  | Stand in front of the screen. |
| Try to face the audience even when writing on a board or chart. |  | Turn your back on the audience. |
| Give the audience time to absorb the information. |  | Read out from the visuals. |
| Have transparencies and slides ready in the correct order. | | |
| Use visuals to build up a picture and use masks, overlays and a pointer. | | |

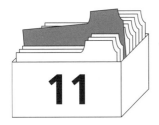

# Content

**11**

The content of your presentation must be suitable for the purpose or objective you are trying to achieve. You should therefore plan the content with this objective in mind.

When you are preparing the content of your presentation, you should think about:

- what to include in your presentation
- structuring the content
- the type of language and vocabulary you will need
- how to prepare your 'lecture notes'
- ways of making your presentation interesting to the audience.

# What should be included in your presentation?

## Collect your thoughts

### Ideas for a presentation to the sales staff of a car manufacturing company

Firstly, gather your thoughts by writing down
ideas on a note pad as you think of them.

You may discover links between items
that you hadn't previously thought of.

You can then organise your
ideas into the order of priority.

# Structuring the main content

Once you have gathered your ideas together, you will need to decide on a structure for your presentation.

You should decide which are the main points that you need to make and in what order. There will also be other points that you wish to discuss that relate to these main points. Deal with them one by one. Generally, audiences find it easier to take in small amounts of information at a time. Do not use long complicated arguments to try to explain several points at once. Break these up with examples.

Here are some examples of how you can organise the information for the main content of your presentation:

## Mind Maps®

Some presenters use **Mind Maps** to help them prepare for a presentation.

Mind Maps can help you to structure your presentation as well as to plan the content of your talk.

In a Mind Map, each main idea or point for your presentation should be drawn as a line or 'branch' from a central box or circle.

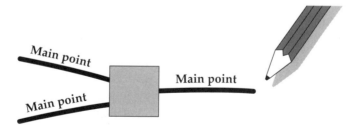

Mind Maps® is a Registered Trade Mark of the Buzan Organisation used with permission.

The secondary points that you will make should be added as 'sub-branch' lines that connect to the main line.

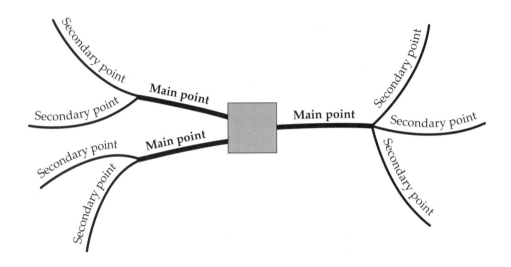

You can add new branches and sub-branches as you think of them. You can also number the main branches on your Mind Map, to show the order in which you will talk about them in your presentation.

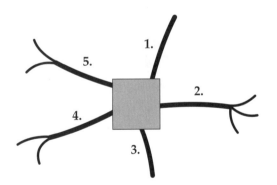

On the opposite page, you will find an example of a diagram for a company presentation at the end of a year. The presenter represents a holding company with subsidiaries dealing in electricity, chemicals and oil.

# A presentation on a company's performance

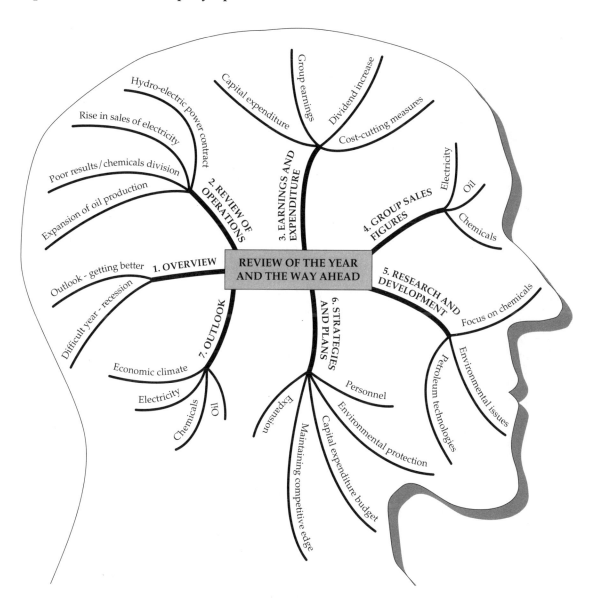

## Prioritise your ideas

Write down all the main points you wish to make in a logical order. This is the 'skeleton' of your presentation. You can then 'flesh out' your ideas with secondary points and examples. Write down these other points as well. They are not absolutely essential but would be worth making if there is enough time. Use a grid like this.

| Subject: Presentation to employees | | |
|---|---|---|
| **Timetable for major new engineering project** | | |
| **1**<br>What **must** be said | **2**<br>What **ought to be** said | **3**<br>What else I **could** say (or omit) if there is (or isn't) time |
| **Importance of the project to the company**<br>Our largest project. | It could be the first of several similar projects. | |
| **Location**<br>Need for some staff to work in another country for up to 12 months.<br>Number of people involved. | Who will be affected.<br>Local labour force. | Information about the country. Our past experience of working in the country. |
| **Stages of the project** | | |
| **Project management**<br>Who will be responsible. | Customer expects completion by December 31st. | We have an excellent record for finishing projects on time. |
| **Practical issues**<br>Installing equipment.<br>Engineering. | Supply of components and raw materials. | Communicating with the customer. Language training. |
| **Conclusion**<br>Confidence of senior management in project team. | | |

Using the grid shown on the previous page, you can prepare three presentations depending on how much time you have.

- Column 1
- Column 1 and 2
- Column 1, 2 and 3. (This includes all the information and would be the preferred choice of presentation.)

See Chapter 8, *Timing*.

If the subject is very complex, you might want to have summaries between the main points.

All your important facts, whether they are advantages and disadvantages, pieces of technical information or statistics should be supported by relevant examples and clear visuals.

## Structuring a presentation: finding a solution

The purpose of a presentation might be to **put forward a solution to a problem (make a recommendation)**. You might be required to give such a presentation as a consultant or adviser when you have been called in by a client to find a solution to a particular problem.

It is sensible to structure this type of presentation in the same way as you would structure a report. This is a common approach in the commercial, technical and scientific world.

Explain the background (or the problem) first, then say how the problem was analysed and give the key findings of your analysis.

Next, look at the possible solutions or options. Compare these options by pointing out the advantages and disadvantages of each. Finally, give the solution that you think is the best one.

British and American presenters usually take this approach to structuring a presentation. They start with the problem and move on to the final result or recommendation. It is an approach which would also work well with an international audience.

Certain nationalities follow different procedures, some starting with the result or recommendation and then working backwards.

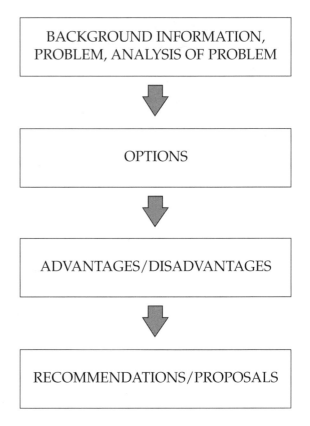

## Structuring a presentation: giving information

The purpose of your presentation might be to speak to your audience about something that is new or unfamiliar to them. You might want to give information about a product or service, for example, or to give some technical information.

In this type of presentation, it will be helpful to work from the known to the unknown. That is, to start with something of which they are already aware and then to move on to the new information.

**Example: presentation about a plan to re-organise a company**

**Stages of the presentation**

1.  The existing structure
    of the company.
2.  Why this structure
    has to be changed.
3.  The new structure.

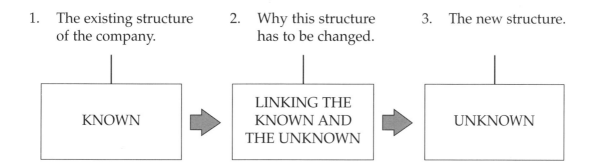

## Language/vocabulary

Make sure you have all the important language and vocabulary you will need to talk about your subject. Your choice of language can help you to make the topic interesting and to draw attention to the key points.

See section, *Putting it into Words* (Chapters 13-32).

## Use spoken English, not written English

Presentations are given orally. They are completely different from written text. Try to use conversational language, not the kind of language you would write in a report. Look at these examples:

 **WRITTEN**

**(More formal, more impersonal)**

 **SPOKEN**

**(More informal, often personal)**

| | |
|---|---|
| To whom do we sell it? | Who do we sell it to? |
| It is recommended that you should... | I think you should... |
| We must now consider... | I'll now turn to... |
| People will, without doubt, have encountered this and will therefore comprehend. | You've all had the same experience and so you know what I mean. |
| I have given some consideration to the problem. | I've given some thought to the problem. |
| Your understanding and cooperation in this matter would be greatly appreciated. | I'd like to ask for your understanding and cooperation in this matter. |

## Note cards

Never write your whole presentation out word for word in full sentences. If you do this, you will not only look down all the time but you will be reading written material aloud, rather than giving a spoken presentation. Your presentation will sound unnatural and impersonal.

In order to stop yourself doing this, make **very brief notes on cards**, only writing down important points or key words.

 You can glance at these note cards quickly but be looking at the audience most of the time while you are speaking. You will also be able to respond to the audience more easily if you are not reading from a script.

**Note cards** should contain:
- key words and phrases
- reminders for when to use visuals
- occasionally, the full text of something you want to read to the audience word for word (e.g. a law or a rule)

You should use one note card for each important point of your presentation.

Note cards should follow the same **structure** of your presentation and will act as reminders of the important things you want to say.

Here is an example:

**NOTE CARD**

**WHAT YOU ACTUALLY SAY**

**ANNUAL SALES**
- graph
- this year/last year
- 12% growth
- target for the next year

I'd now like to look at our sales figures and compare this year's figures with those of last year. You can see from this graph that we achieved record sales this year. Compared with last year, there was a twelve per cent rise. We can feel justifiably proud of our sales performance but we mustn't become complacent. Now, turning to our target for the coming year,...

Note cards should be readable at a glance. Reduce words to a minimum and use a large typeface. You can also include graphics, for example, a flowchart could help you to remember a sequence of ideas.

Number the cards in sequence to help you follow the structure you have planned for your presentation. (If you drop any, you will be able to find your place quickly.) You can also write down how long each card should take to help you keep to the time available for your presentation.

# Make your presentation interesting to the audience

Audience attention is focused at the beginning of a presentation but often drops after the first part so you need to keep them interested in your talk. Here are some ways to create interest in your presentation:

- **Rhetorical questions** can be used for dramatic effect and to keep the audience's attention by involving them in solving problems. Rhetorical questions are questions to which you do not expect to get an answer. You will answer the questions yourself but while you pause, the audience will be thinking of their own answers and therefore focus on what you are trying to say.

- You can introduce variety into your talk by using **visuals**. If you use too many or

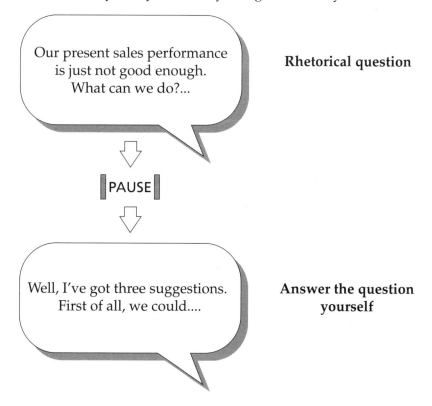

Our present sales performance is just not good enough. What can we do?...

**Rhetorical question**

PAUSE

Well, I've got three suggestions. First of all, we could....

**Answer the question yourself**

too few visuals in your presentation, the audience may become bored.

- Try not to have very long and complicated arguments or to talk in the abstract without giving **examples**. Examples of actual events are more interesting rather than general theories with nothing to back them up. The audience will feel more involved if you talk about ideas and situations that are relevant to them or that they have experienced.

- You can appeal to the audience's **curiosity**. If you promise to provide them with something that interests them, they will listen to you. For example, you could begin a presentation on sales techniques by saying, 'I am going to tell you how to double your sales figures by making half the usual number of calls'.

- Some presenters use relevant **anecdotes, jokes and quotations** to make their talks interesting. All these are fine, providing that they are not over-used and that you have taken into account any possible cultural taboos and linguistic misunderstandings if you are talking to an international audience.

For information on preparing and using visuals see Chapter 9,
*Preparing Visuals* and Chapter 10, *Using Visuals*.

For the language to use for rhetorical questions see Chapter 22,
*Involving the audience*, 'Using rhetorical questions'.

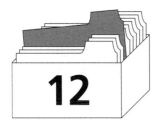

# Structure

**12**

In Chapter 11 we looked at how you should organise the main content of the presentation. However, a presentation also has an overall structure. In this chapter we look at what you should say in the different parts of the presentation.

Most presentations follow this sequence:

When planning your presentation, remember that the introduction, summary and conclusion should be brief. The **main content** should take the longest amount of time.

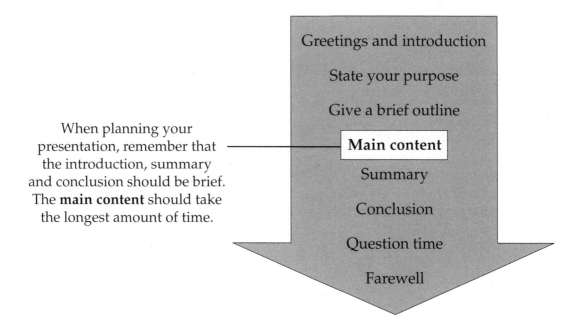

Greetings and introduction

State your purpose

Give a brief outline

**Main content**

Summary

Conclusion

Question time

Farewell

## Greetings and introduction

If there is no one else to introduce you at the start of your presentation, you should **greet the audience** and **introduce yourself**. In your introduction you should tell them something about yourself, your company or your responsibilities, whatever is relevant to the presentation.

For language, see Chapter 18, *Beginning the presentation*, 'Greeting the audience and introducing yourself'.

It is useful, before you start, to tell the audience when you will deal with questions, either during or after the talk.

For language, see Chapter 19, *Stating the purpose, giving an outline*, 'Saying when you will deal with questions'.

It is also helpful for the audience to know whether they will receive handouts or whether they will need to copy your visuals, etc. You will be more likely to have the audience's attention if they know they can just sit and listen without having to make notes.

For language, see Chapter 20, *Referring to handouts* and Chapter 28, *Referring to visuals*.

Don't start your introduction until the audience has settled down and you have got everyone's attention.

## Stating the purpose and giving an outline of the presentation

After your introduction, tell the audience the **subject** and **purpose** of your presentation. This focuses the audience's attention on what you are going to talk about and why.

Then, give them a **brief outline** of what you are going to say. This means telling them in which order you will deal with different items. You should give an overview of your key points so the audience will understand better what follows.

Your outline should

- get audience attention and focus it on your theme
- give an overview of the key points of your presentation
- tell them the content and structure of your presentation

The attention of the people in the audience is at its peak at the beginning of the presentation. A strong opening can attract and keep their interest. One way of doing this is to make a statement that will appeal to their needs and the main reason why they are attending the presentation. For example, 'Did you know that most companies spend more on entertaining than on staff training?'.

## Main content

This is the most important part of the presentation when you will give the audience the vital information about your subject. You should make the subject as clear and interesting as possible for the audience. State your most important points in a logical order and always give examples and evidence to support your opinions.

This is covered in more detail in Chapter 11, *Content*.

## Summary and conclusion

### Summary

When you have finished the main part, you should then summarise your presentation.

The closing lines should convey the same message as the outline that introduced your presentation but be expressed differently. Try also to end on an interesting point so that the audience will feel positive or inspired at the end of your presentation.

Let the audience know that you are about to end. This will help their attention to rise again and they will listen to any important points in your summary. They may have missed one or two points in the middle of your presentation and will now have a chance to hear them again.

Your summary should:

- briefly remind the audience of what has been said
- re-cap all the main points of the presentation
- be memorable. (These will be the last words of your presentation.)
- say or suggest what you expect your audience to do, believe or know, etc. as a result of your talk. (The purpose.)

Do not summarise a very short presentation, it will seem repetitive.

## Conclusion

Conclude the presentation by thanking the audience for listening and invite them to ask questions.

See Chapter 30, *Summarising and concluding.*

## Dealing with questions

You can find out whether the audience has understood what you have been talking about in your presentation and whether you have covered all they need to know by the way they respond in question and answer sessions.

If you know something about the audience and their needs, you can try to anticipate any possible questions they might ask. You can prepare your answers or cover those points in your talk.

Listen carefully to a question. Ask for **clarification** rather than trying to answer a question when you are unsure about its meaning.

## Clarifying questions

One particular worry for presenters speaking in a foreign language is 'Will I understand the question?'. This can also be a problem for native-speaker presenters as people often ask complicated questions or do not phrase their questions clearly.

- You can ask the questioner to **re-phrase** the question.
- You can try to **break down** a long complicated question into several shorter points.
- You can also **repeat** what you think the question is and ask the questioner to confirm whether your understanding is correct or not.

| | |
|---|---|
| • You can delay answering a question to give yourself more thinking time. | • You can give a more indirect answer to a question. |
| • You can ask for clarification; ask the questioner to repeat the question in different words. | • If you honestly don't know the answer to a question, say that you can't answer that question at the moment but that you will try to find out the answer later on. If people ask a whole series of questions in one go, answer each question separately. |

| DO! | | DON'T! |
|---|---|---|
| Stick to the allotted time. | ⬌ | Run over time. |
| Begin when you have everyone's attention. | ⬌ | Start while people are still talking or moving about. |
| Introduce yourself and give an outline of your talk. | ⬌ | Start immediately on the main part. |
| Use humour if relevant. | ⬌ | Tell jokes or anecdotes which may embarrass or cause misunderstanding. |
| Clarify your understanding of questions before you answer them. | ⬌ | Answer a question you are unsure about. |
| Keep cool under pressure. | ⬌ | Become aggressive or defensive. |
| Tell them they will receive handouts. | | |
| Order your presentation logically. | | |
| Work from the known to the unknown. | | |
| Summarise what you have said. | | |

**Answering questions**

# Putting it into Words

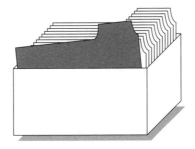

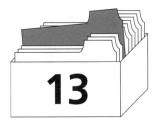

# Preparing the main message

**13**

When you are about to give a presentation, one of the most useful things to do is to prepare a list of words that you will need to deliver your message. Rather than just making a long list of words, you should try to group them together. In this section, you will find information on:

 **key words**

 **word families**

 words and phrases to use when talking about **trends**

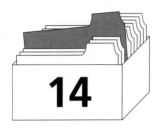

# Key words

## 14

It is helpful to consider the **key words** that you will need for your presentation. If you are giving a presentation about production, 'production' will be one of your key words. Remind yourself of other words that are often used with 'production' to make a word partnership. Some of these words go in front of 'production', some go after it, for example, 'automated production' and 'production manager'.

 **Production**

| just-in-time<br>automated<br>efficient | PRODUCTION | line<br>flow<br>capacity<br>budget<br>schedule<br>delay<br>manager<br>methods<br>machinery |
|---|---|---|

## Examples

**Automated production** often includes the use of robots.
The **production budget** is normally agreed at the end of the previous year.
Every company should have **efficient production** methods.

 Sales

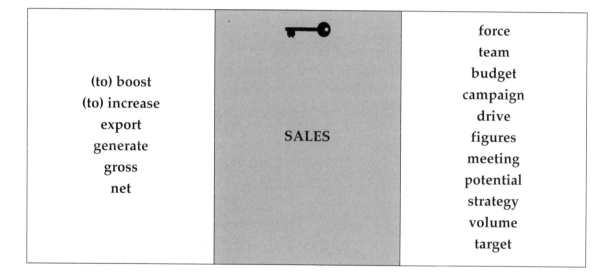

| (to) boost (to) increase export generate gross net | **SALES** | force team budget campaign drive figures meeting potential strategy volume target |
|---|---|---|

## Examples

The new advertising campaign should **boost sales** considerably.
The **sales potential** of this product in the US is enormous.
The **sales team** will easily reach its **export sales target** this year.

 ## Profit

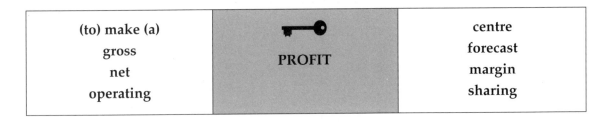

| (to) make (a)<br>gross<br>net<br>operating | PROFIT | centre<br>forecast<br>margin<br>sharing |
|---|---|---|

### Examples

The company **made** a considerable **profit** last year.
We intend to introduce a **profit sharing** scheme for our staff.
The **net profit** after tax was £550 million.

 ## Research

| medical<br>scientific | RESEARCH | work<br>scientist<br>programme<br>project<br>and development |
|---|---|---|

## Examples

We have set up a new **research and development department**.
The government has increased its spending on **medical research**.
The **research programme** will finish in two years' time.

 **Price**

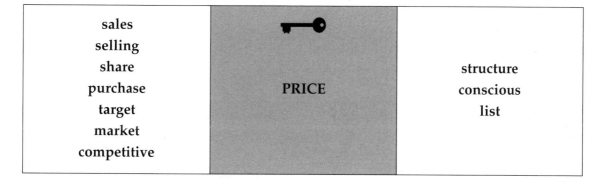

| | | |
|---|---|---|
| sales | | structure |
| selling | | conscious |
| share | | list |
| purchase | PRICE | |
| target | | |
| market | | |
| competitive | | |

## Examples

The **share price** went up ten per cent yesterday.
Our customers are very **price conscious**.
We charge a **competitive price** for our products.

Here are some blank forms to help you think of key words to use in the main part of your presentation. You can then write some sentences for your presentation, using some of the word partnerships.

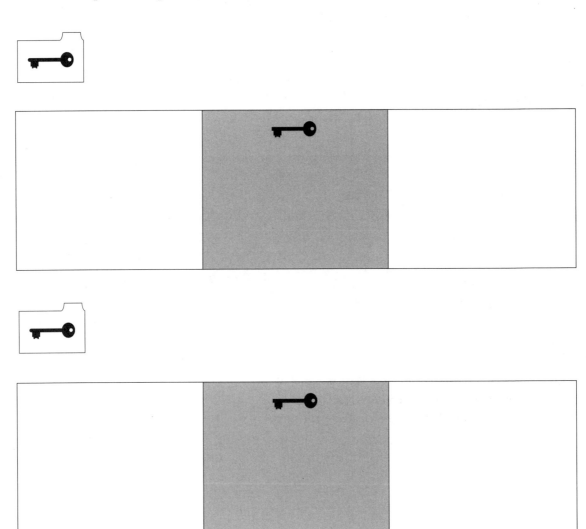

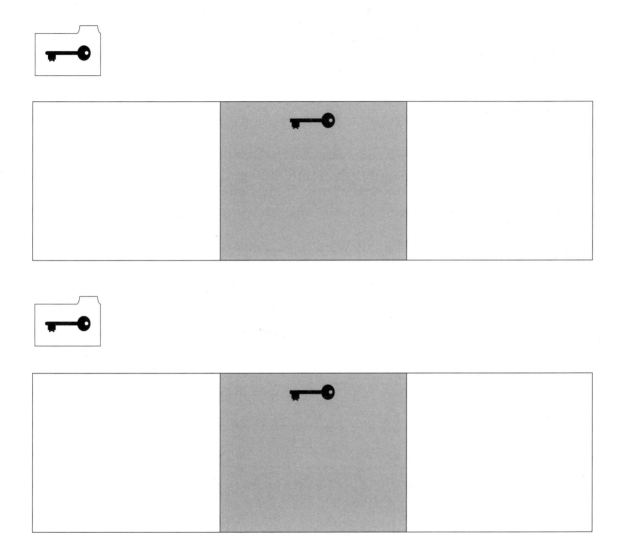

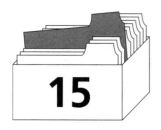

# Word families

**15**

If you make a note of any derivatives (word families) you may need in your presentation, then you will not make the common mistake of using a noun instead of an adjective.

**Examples**

Here is an example of a presenter using the word family below:

> 'Turning now to the **competition**, as you know, we have three main **competitors**, one of which is Masons who have managed to maintain their **competitive** advantage in the export market.'

| NOUN(S) | VERB | ADJECTIVE |
|---|---|---|
| competition<br>competitor | (to) compete | competitive |

| NOUN(S) | VERB | ADJECTIVE |
|---|---|---|
| product<br>production<br>productivity<br>producer | (to) produce | productive |

| NOUN(S) | VERB | ADJECTIVE |
|---|---|---|
| profit<br>profitability | (to) profit<br>(to) make a profit | profitable |

You can use the boxes below to write down some word families which you may need for your presentation:

| NOUN(S) | VERB | ADJECTIVE |
|---------|------|-----------|
|         |      |           |

| NOUN(S) | VERB | ADJECTIVE |
|---------|------|-----------|
|         |      |           |

| NOUN(S) | VERB | ADJECTIVE |
|---------|------|-----------|
|         |      |           |

| NOUN(S) | VERB | ADJECTIVE |
|---------|------|-----------|
|         |      |           |

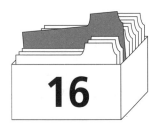

# Talking about trends

**16**

In presentations to shareholders, sales presentations and those related to financial matters, it is often necessary to refer to trends. In this chapter you will find some words to describe trends. They are particularly useful when referring to visuals.

 **Upward trends**

You may be talking about annual profit, an increase in sales, costs, demands, etc. Here are some examples of how you can refer to a visual which is showing an upward trend.

**Example 1**

As you can see from this graph, there was a **significant increase** in sales during the first half of this year.

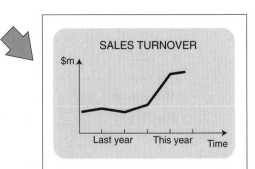

## Example 2

> If you look at this graph, you will see that short-term interest rates **rose** during the first half of this year and peaked at 6%.

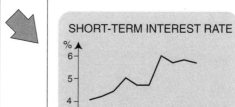

| VERBS | NOUNS |
|:---:|:---:|
| (to) go up | |
| (to) climb | |
| (to) rise | (a) rise |
| (to) increase | (an) increase |
| (to) grow | growth |
| (to) peak/reach a peak | (a) peak |
| (to) improve/pick up | (an) improvement |
| (to) expand | (an) expansion |
| (to) boom | (a) boom |
| (to) recover | (a) recovery |

**Downward Trends**

## Example

As you can see from this chart, output at our plant in Germany **fell** by 200,000 units last year compared with the previous year.

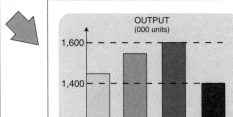

| VERBS | NOUNS |
|---|---|
| (to) go down | |
| (to) fall | (a) fall |
| (to) drop | (a) drop |
| (to) decrease | (a) decrease |
| (to) decline | (a) decline |
| (to) collapse | (a) collapse |
| (to) slump | (a) slump |
| (to) shrink | |
| (to) bottom out | |

## To indicate stability and change

**Example**

In 1990, our share of the market stood at ten per cent. Since then, it has **risen steadily** and is now nearly twenty per cent.

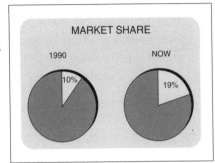

| STABILITY | CHANGE |
|---|---|
| (to) stand at<br>(to) remain constant<br>(a) remain stable/the same | (to) level off<br>(to) recover/pick up<br>(to) fall off<br>(to) fluctuate |

**To indicate speed and size of change**

**Example**

 I'd like you to have a look at this graph which shows that consumer spending **increased significantly** after the cuts in taxation.

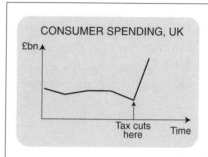

| ADJECTIVES | ADVERBS |
|---|---|
| **SPEED**<br>rapid/slow<br>sudden/gradual | **SPEED**<br>rapidly/slowly<br>suddenly/gradually |
| **SIZE**<br>sharp/steady<br>considerable/slight<br>dramatic<br>substantial<br>significant | **SIZE**<br>sharply/steadily<br>considerably/slightly<br>dramatically<br>substantially<br>significantly |

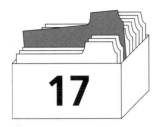

# Presentation phrases

**17**

The following Chapters 18-32 show you some phrases that you can use in a presentation, to let your audience know what you are going to say or to focus their attention.

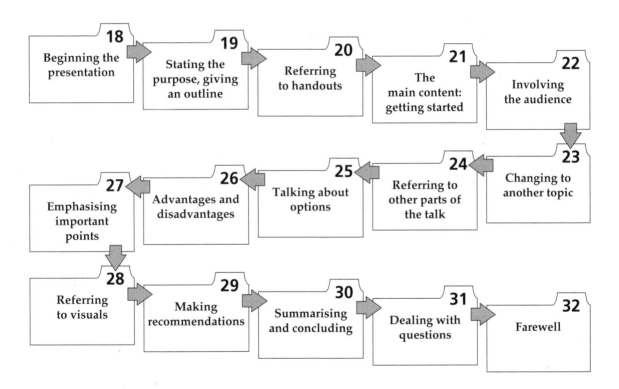

**18** Beginning the presentation

**19** Stating the purpose, giving an outline

**20** Referring to handouts

**21** The main content: getting started

**22** Involving the audience

**23** Changing to another topic

**24** Referring to other parts of the talk

**25** Talking about options

**26** Advantages and disadvantages

**27** Emphasising important points

**28** Referring to visuals

**29** Making recommendations

**30** Summarising and concluding

**31** Dealing with questions

**32** Farewell

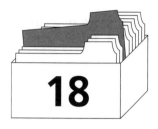

# Beginning the presentation

## 18

Before you begin your presentation, you should greet the audience and for an external presentation, say who you are and which company you represent. You may wish to add more information about your experience or qualifications.

**Greeting the audience and introducing yourself**

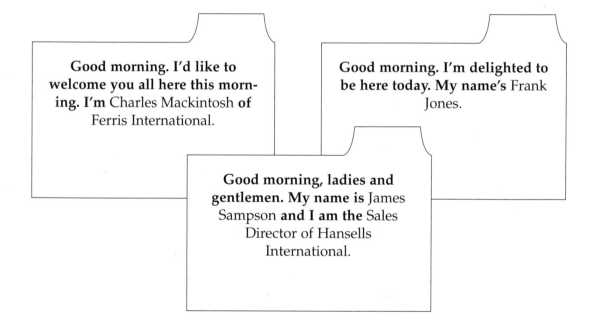

**Good morning. I'd like to welcome you all here this morning. I'm** Charles Mackintosh **of** Ferris International.

**Good morning. I'm delighted to be here today. My name's** Frank Jones.

**Good morning, ladies and gentlemen. My name is** James Sampson **and I am the** Sales Director of Hansells International.

Good morning everyone. I'm Alan Gillingham of Frasers and I'm grateful for the opportunity to present our new product to you.

Good morning, everyone. Thank you all for coming. Let me introduce myself. My name's Rebecca Mason and I am from Gregson PLC.

## Saying something about yourself

Before I carry on, let me tell you something about myself. I've been working for Simpsons for fifteen years.

My experience in this field began in 1980 when I joined a large engineering firm.

# Welcoming the audience

Welcome to Baxters. **Thank you for giving me the opportunity to talk to you today.**

**Thank you for inviting me to speak to you today.**

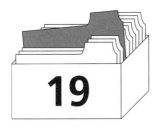

# Stating the purpose, giving an outline

**19**

After the introduction, you should tell the audience the purpose of your presentation and give them a brief outline of the talk. It is also a good idea to tell them how long you intend to take.

## Stating the purpose

**What I'd like to do today is to** present our new list of client services.

**As you know, I'm here today to talk about** our latest product.

**The purpose of my talk is to** present a proposal for the new production site.

**In my presentation** this morning, **I'll be** reviewing our sales performance over the last six months.

I'm grateful for the opportunity to make this sales presentation to you.

I'm going to be talking about the recent market survey.

I wanted to take this opportunity to explain to you the changes we are planning for the company and why they are neccessary.

## Giving an outline of your presentation

I'll start by telling you who we are and what we do, then we'll look at what the customer needs from us and I'll explain how we can meet those needs. Finally, I'll give you our prices and show you that we represent value for money.

As you know, I'm here to suggest some solutions to the problem. I'll first of all outline the methods we used to establish the causes of the problem, then I'll discuss our findings, and finally, we'll look at alternative solutions and I'll make a recommendation.

**I have divided my talk into three main parts:**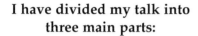

**firstly,** I'd like to remind you of how things looked at this time last year,

**secondly,** I'll discuss our performance over the last six months,

**and, finally,** I'll look at our target for the next six months.

**I'll begin with** some general comments about the company **and then I'll deal with** each department in turn. **After that, we'll look at** future trends.

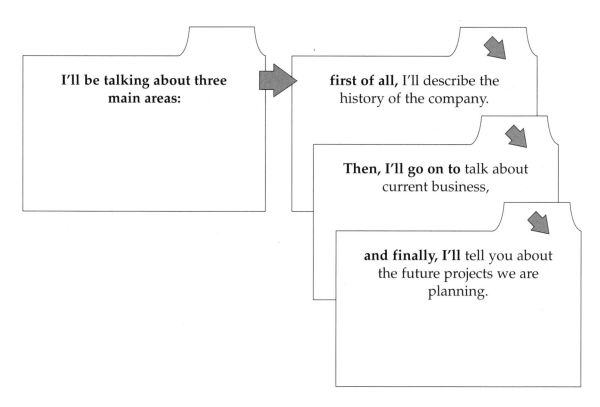

I'll be talking about three main areas:

**first of all,** I'll describe the history of the company.

**Then, I'll go on to** talk about current business,

**and finally, I'll** tell you about the future projects we are planning.

## Saying how long you will take

**I'll only take about** thirty minutes or so of your time.

## Saying when you will deal with questions

If you don't mind, I'll deal with questions at the end of my talk.

Please feel free to interrupt at any time if you'd like to ask a question.

See also Chapter 31, *Dealing with questions.*

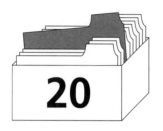

# Referring to handouts

**20**

Handouts can make a presentation easier for the audience as they can listen without making notes. Let the audience know at the beginning of the presentation whether you will be giving them handouts or copies of any visuals.

**There's no need for you to take notes. At the end of the presentation, I'll give you a complete set of handouts containing all the important points.**

**You needn't copy any of the visuals, I'll give you copies of everything later on.**

**I hope you all have a copy of my handout. It contains** all the visuals I will be using.

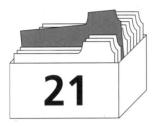

# The main content: getting started

## 21

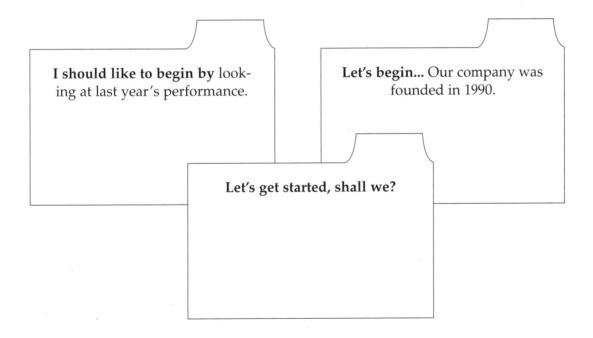

I should like to begin by looking at last year's performance.

Let's begin... Our company was founded in 1990.

Let's get started, shall we?

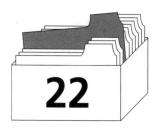

# Involving the audience

**22**

It is important to make the audience feel involved. You can do this by asking rhetorical questions and by referring to the audience personally.

## Using rhetorical questions

Supposing you lost one of your biggest clients. **How would you deal with this?**

This campaign was unsuccessful. **And what did we learn from this?** We learnt not to be complacent.

Over the last two years, there has been a considerable drop in profits. **What was the reason for this?** Obviously, the economic recession throughout Europe was a key factor.

It has been decided to make some structural changes in the company. **How will this affect our department?** Well, unfortunately, it will result in some redundancies.

As you can see, our products really meet the needs of today's market. **How do we manage to do all this at such a low cost?** Well,...

There is a great demand for this type of product in Japan. **What, then, are the implications for** our company? Well, we intend to appoint local agents in Tokyo.

**So, why are we losing customers to our competitor?** I think our delivery service is much too slow.

If you look at this chart, you will see that this study has taken far longer than we would have liked. **How can we explain this?** First of all, the initial research took much longer than expected.

## Referring to the audience personally

I'm sure you'll all agree with me that we must make a greater effort to improve our sales performance in central Europe.

You will all be aware of the project that has been carried out by the Research and Development department.

Some of you may have had a similar experience yourselves.

Did you know that we have already sold one million of these items so far this year?

I hope you will understand that these changes are necessary if we are to move forward.

There have been tremendous problems in this industry for the last five years. You will all know what I mean.

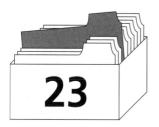

# Changing to another topic

**23**

The audience will find it easier to follow your presentation if you make it clear when you are changing the subject.

So, we've looked at the various problems and **I'd now like to consider** some possible solutions.

Having looked at all the possible options, **let's move on** to the advantages and disadvantages of each one.

**This leads me to my next point which is** the question of attracting more investment.

**Moving on now** to the environmental question. We are taking every precaution to ensure the careful disposal of waste.

**So**, I'm sure you will agree that this is a really exciting new product. **Now**, turning to our prices.

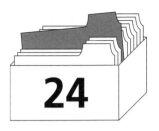

# Referring to other parts of the talk

**24**

Sometimes, you need to refer to something you mentioned earlier or will come back to later.

**I'd like to go back to a point I mentioned earlier,** the performance of our latest brand.

**As I've already said**, increasing our market share is one of our top priorities for the coming year.

Next year's prices will only be two per cent higher than this year's. **I'll come back to this point in a moment.**

**Let's just re-cap** on that point.

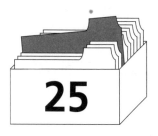

# Talking about options

**25**

You may sometimes wish to discuss two or more possible options.

As I see it, **there are two possible options open to us. One is** to establish a branch in the Ukraine immediately. **The other is** to send out representatives from our Moscow operation.

**What are the options open to us? Well, we could** modify the existing model. **Alternatively,** we could consider developing a new one.

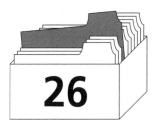

# **Advantages and disadvantages**

## 26

You mention the positive and negative aspects of one or more options by referring to their advantages and disadvantages.

I've outlined three possible courses of action. Now, **what are the advantages** of each one? Well, **I tend to favour** the first option **because** expenditure will be lower.

**The benefit of** relocating to the Far East is the better access to raw materials. **Other advantages are** that labour is cheaper and, in general, the facilities are better. **The disadvantages are** the poor location and the currency risk.

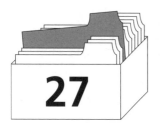

# Emphasising important points

**27**

Using adverbs in front of adjectives makes the adjectives stronger and helps to emphasise important points.

## Using adverbs with adjectives

The success of this campaign is **extremely important** to the company.

The increase in consumer spending over the last year is **highly significant**.

So, I think it is **extremely dangerous** to assume that, because we have been successful up to now, we will continue to be so. We can't be complacent.

The release of toxic chemicals into the environment is **totally unacceptable** to us.

# Other ways of emphasising key points

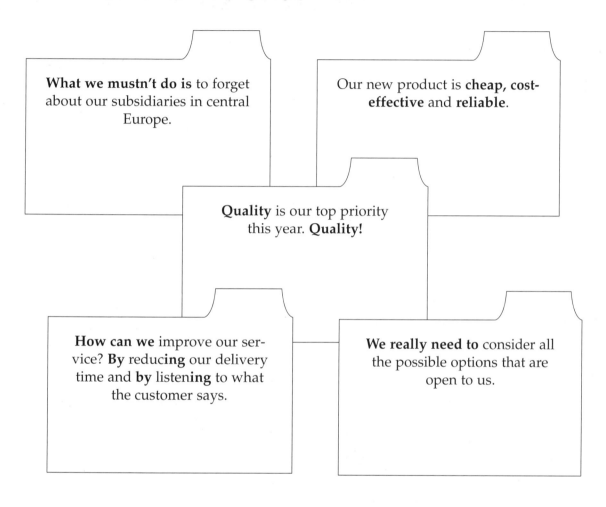

What **we mustn't do is** to forget about our subsidiaries in central Europe.

Our new product is **cheap, cost-effective** and **reliable**.

**Quality** is our top priority this year. **Quality!**

**How can we** improve our service? **By** redu**c**ing our delivery time and **by** listen**ing** to what the customer says.

**We really need to** consider all the possible options that are open to us.

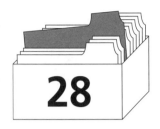

# Referring to visuals

**28**

You should give the audience a 'signal' when you are about to show them a visual. This helps them to focus on the important information.

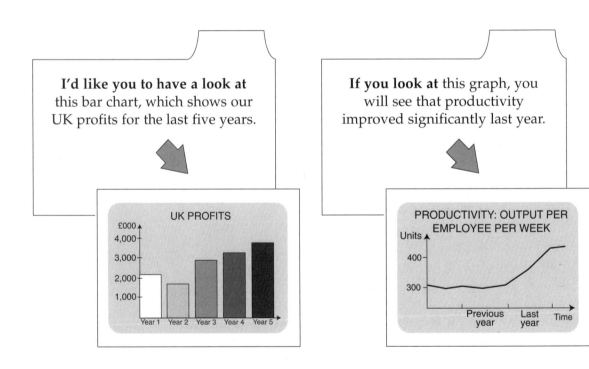

**I'd like you to have a look at** this bar chart, which shows our UK profits for the last five years.

UK PROFITS

£000
4,000
3,000
2,000
1,000

Year 1  Year 2  Year 3  Year 4  Year 5

**If you look at** this graph, you will see that productivity improved significantly last year.

PRODUCTIVITY: OUTPUT PER EMPLOYEE PER WEEK

Units

400
300

Previous year    Last year    Time

**The figures in this table show** how the number of employees in this company has grown over the past ten years. As you will see, staff numbers have almost tripled in ten years.

| Number of Employees (000s) | | | |
|---|---|---|---|
| | 10 years ago | 5 years ago | Now |
| Manufacturing | 75 | 100 | 140 |
| Marketing | 120 | 250 | 410 |
| Administration | 105 | 150 | 320 |
| Total | 300 | 500 | 870 |

**As you can see from** this pie chart, we have a twenty-five per cent share of the total market at the moment.

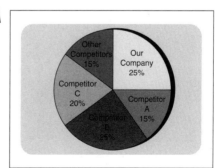

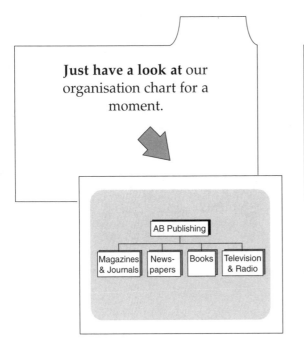

**Just have a look at** our organisation chart for a moment.

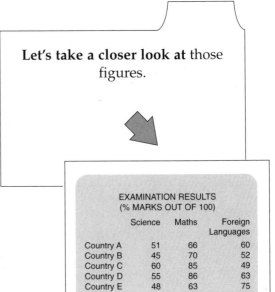

**Let's take a closer look at** those figures.

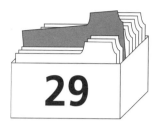

# 29 Making recommendations

You may sometimes wish to make recommendations to the audience.

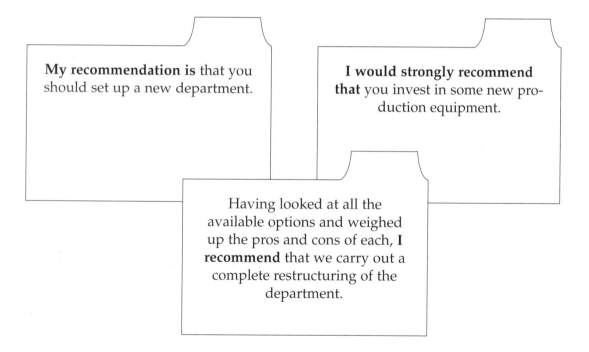

**My recommendation is** that you should set up a new department.

**I would strongly recommend that** you invest in some new production equipment.

Having looked at all the available options and weighed up the pros and cons of each, **I recommend** that we carry out a complete restructuring of the department.

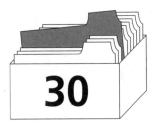

**30**

# Summarising and concluding

It is very important to summarise the most important points before you conclude your presentation.

## Summarising

I'm now nearing the end of my talk and, **at this stage, I'd like to run through my main points again.**

**To sum up then,** we must reduce our personnel costs, and to do this, we must cut the size of the workforce.

**To summarise the main points of my talk,** we have to become more competitive. We must also consider the development of new products. Finally, we have to be more profitable.

# Concluding

**I'd like to conclude by** reminding you of something I said at the beginning of my talk.

**That brings me to the end of my presentation,** ladies and gentlemen. I hope you found it interesting. **I'd like to thank you all for your attention.**

**Thank you all for listening.** I hope you will agree that our new product is exciting and innovative. Please contact me if you need further information.

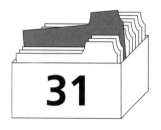

# Dealing with questions

**31**

At the end of the presentation you should invite the audience to ask questions. There are various ways to respond.

## Inviting questions

I'd like to thank you for your attention. **Now, if there are any questions, I'll be pleased to answer them.**

Thank you all for listening. **If you have any questions, I'll do my best to answer them.**

# Clarifying questions before answering

> Sorry, could you say that again, please?

> I'm sorry. I didn't hear you. Would you mind repeating your question?

> **If I've understood your question correctly, you would like me to explain** the criteria we used to choose the bases for our European operations.

> **When you say** South America, **do you mean** South America generally, or Brazil, where we are at present?

# Avoiding giving an answer

> I'm afraid I'm not the right person to give you an answer to that question.

> I'm afraid I'm not able to answer that question at present. If you'd like to leave me your phone number, I'll try to get back to you on that.

## Showing tactful disagreement

Yes, I see your point but I know **you will appreciate** how important it is to keep up to date with the latest technology.

Well, I have some doubts about that.

## Giving reassurance

Clearly, that's very important **but...**

I can understand your concern **but** we will be creating new jobs in other departments.

You need have no worries on that point. I can assure you that proper safety precautions will be carried out.

## Answering questions during a presentation

(In response to an interruption)
**If you wouldn't mind waiting,
I'd prefer to answer your
question later on.**

(Inviting questions in the middle
of your presentation)
**Before I go on to the next part
of my presentation, are there
any questions on what I've
said so far?**

**19**

See also Chapter 19, *Stating the purpose, giving an outline*, 'Saying when you will deal with questions'.

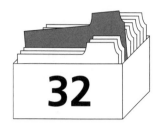

# Farewell

**32**

Finally, it is important to thank the audience for listening.

**Are there any more questions? No? Well, in that case, thank you again for your attention** and I'd like to remind you to pick up a copy of the handouts on your way out.

**If there are no more questions, thank you for your interest.** I look forward to seeing you again next year.

**So, all that remains is for me to thank you again for listening and to wish you a good journey home.**

# Evaluating the Presentation

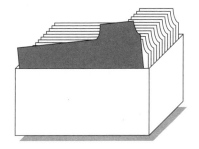

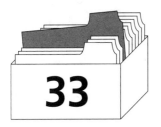

# Before the presentation

## 33

These checklists will help you to prepare your presentation.

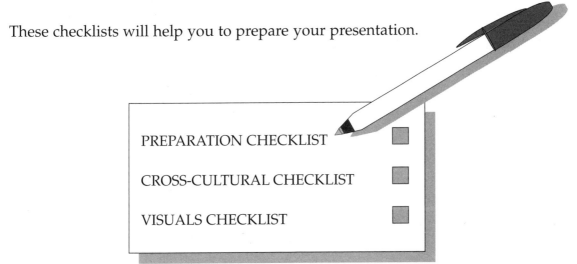

PREPARATION CHECKLIST ☐

CROSS-CULTURAL CHECKLIST ☐

VISUALS CHECKLIST ☐

## Preparation checklist

Have you prepared everything? It may help to use the following checklist to remind yourself of important points.

## PREPARATION CHECKLIST

**Subject of presentation**

**My objectives**

| | | |
|---|---|---|
| Educate/train ☐ | Inform/explain ☐ |
| Persuade ☐ | Give instructions ☐ |
| Sell something ☐ | |

**Audience profile**

| | Good | Some | Poor |
|---|---|---|---|
| Knowledge of the subject | ☐ | ☐ | ☐ |

| | Large | Small |
|---|---|---|
| Size of audience | ☐ | ☐ |

| | Formal | Informal |
|---|---|---|
| Formality | ☐ | ☐ |

| | Friendly | Unfriendly |
|---|---|---|
| Attitude | ☐ | ☐ |

**Content and structure**

| | Yes | No |
|---|---|---|
| Have I planned the content and structure? | ☐ | ☐ |
| Have I prepared my notes? | ☐ | ☐ |

## PREPARATION CHECKLIST (Continued)

Key points to be covered

|                                                    | Yes | No |
|----------------------------------------------------|-----|-----|
| **Closure**                                        |     |     |
| Have I planned how I shall end the presentation?   | ☐   | ☐   |

|                                                    | Yes | No |
|----------------------------------------------------|-----|-----|
| **Visuals**                                        |     |     |
| Do I need visuals?                                 | ☐   | ☐   |
| Have I planned what they should be?                | ☐   | ☐   |
| Have they been prepared?                           | ☐   | ☐   |

|                                                    | Yes | No |
|----------------------------------------------------|-----|-----|
| **Equipment**                                      |     |     |
| Have I checked that it is available?               | ☐   | ☐   |
| The equipment I need is:                           |     |     |

## PREPARATION CHECKLIST (Continued)

Timing                    Length of presentation    [    ]  minutes
                          Time for questions        [    ]  minutes

Handouts                                                    Yes   No

    Do I need handouts?                          [  ]  [  ]

    Have they been prepared?                     [  ]  [  ]

Questions

    What questions might be asked by the audience?

# Cross-cultural checklist

You can use this checklist to help you prepare for a presentation to people from a different culture. Look at the list overleaf and think about any possible differences between your own culture and the culture of your audience.

If you would like to find out more about the cultural background of a particular audience, you could ask a colleague who has given presentations to audiences from that culture or read as much information as you can.

It is also useful to ask someone from that culture about what is acceptable and what is unacceptable when giving presentations. It is important to avoid saying or doing things which will offend or cause you or your audience embarrassment.

# CROSS-CULTURAL CHECKLIST

| | Your culture | The culture of your audience |
|---|---|---|
| Wear formal clothes | Yes ☐  No ☐ | Yes ☐  No ☐ |
| Make jokes | Yes ☐  No ☐ | Yes ☐  No ☐ |
| Ask the audience questions | Yes ☐  No ☐ | Yes ☐  No ☐ |
| Keep to the allotted time | Yes ☐  No ☐ | Yes ☐  No ☐ |
| Make provocative statements | Yes ☐  No ☐ | Yes ☐  No ☐ |
| Maintain eye contact | Yes ☐  No ☐ | Yes ☐  No ☐ |

# Visuals checklist

Use this checklist for your visuals before giving your presentation. Check each visual separately.

## VISUALS CHECKLIST

| | Yes | No |
|---|---|---|
| Am I happy with the way the visual looks? | ☐ | ☐ |
| Is there too much information on the visual? | ☐ | ☐ |
| Is there enough information on the visual? | ☐ | ☐ |
| Is the information clear and logically presented? | ☐ | ☐ |
| Are there any mistakes on the visual? | ☐ | ☐ |
| Will the audience be able to read the visual? | ☐ | ☐ |
| Will the audience understand what the visual shows? | ☐ | ☐ |
| Do the diagrams explain what I am saying? | ☐ | ☐ |
| Have I used symbols to good effect? | ☐ | ☐ |
| Does the visual make good use of colour? | ☐ | ☐ |
| Do I need to change the visual? | ☐ | ☐ |

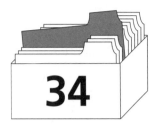

# Giving the presentation

**34**

You cannot complete a checklist in the middle of giving a presentation! However, there are some questions that you should be asking yourself while talking to the audience. Try to remember them when you stand up to begin speaking.

Do they understand what I am saying?

Am I speaking too quickly?

Do they look interested?

Are they bored?

Have I talked for too long without showing a visual?

Do I need a change of emphasis?

Are they getting tired?

Am I keeping to the time?

Although you have prepared your presentation carefully, you should be sensitive to the

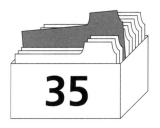

# After the presentation

**35**

Complete these evaluation sheets **after** you have given your presentation. They will help you to decide whether your presentation was successful, and whether you can improve your performance the next time you give a presentation.

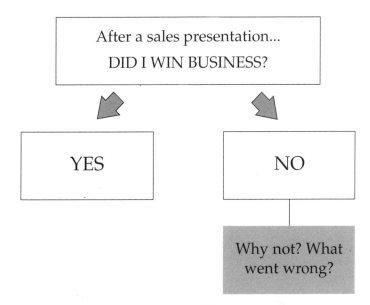

## CHECKLIST: HOW GOOD WAS MY PRESENTATION?

Purpose/objectives

    Did I achieve my objectives?

                    Yes ☐

                    No ☐

                    I don't know ☐

    Did the audience like the presentation?

                    Very much ☐

                    Yes ☐

                    A little ☐

                    No ☐

                    I don't know ☐

    What went well?

    What did not go very well?

## CHECKLIST: HOW GOOD WAS MY PRESENTATION? (Continued)

My performance

| | | |
|---|---|---|
| Did I make myself understood? | Yes | ☐ |
| | I think so | ☐ |
| | Not very well | ☐ |
| | I don't know | ☐ |
| | | |
| Did I have difficulty with my English? | No | ☐ |
| | A little | ☐ |
| | Yes | ☐ |
| | | |
| Did I speak clearly? | Yes | ☐ |
| Did I use my voice well? | Some of the time | ☐ |
| | No | ☐ |
| | | |
| Did I use good body language? | Yes | ☐ |
| | No | ☐ |

What should I try to do better next time?

## CHECKLIST: HOW GOOD WAS MY PRESENTATION? (Continued)

| | Yes | No |
|---|---|---|
| **Structure** | | |
| Did I state the purpose of my presentation? | ☐ | ☐ |
| Did I explain the sequence of my presentation? | ☐ | ☐ |
| **Content** | | |
| Did I emphasise important points? | ☐ | ☐ |
| Did I signal when the audience should look at visuals? | ☐ | ☐ |
| Did I make my recommendations clear? | ☐ | ☐ |
| Did I involve the audience? | ☐ | ☐ |
| **Summary** | | |
| Did I summarise the main points at the end? | ☐ | ☐ |
| **Questions** | | |
| Did I deal well with the questions? | ☐ | ☐ |
| **Visuals** | | |
| Did I explain them well? | ☐ | ☐ |
| **Timing** | | |
| Did I time the presentation well? | ☐ | ☐ |
| Did I have time to say everything? | ☐ | ☐ |

## CHECKLIST: HOW GOOD WAS MY PRESENTATION? (Continued)

Action points

Is there anything I should do as a result of the presentation?

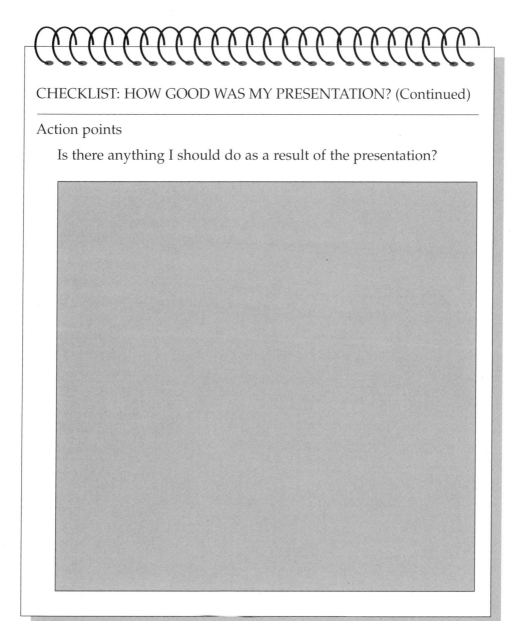